HAPPY
Valentine's Day

WE HOPE WE CAN GET POSITIVE FEEDBACK FROM YOU ON OUR PRODUCT ON AMAZON.

THIS BOOK

Belongs To

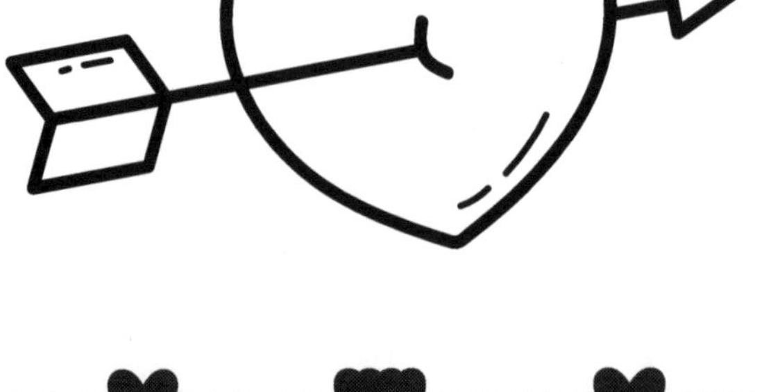

TEST COLOR PAGE

I LOVE YOU

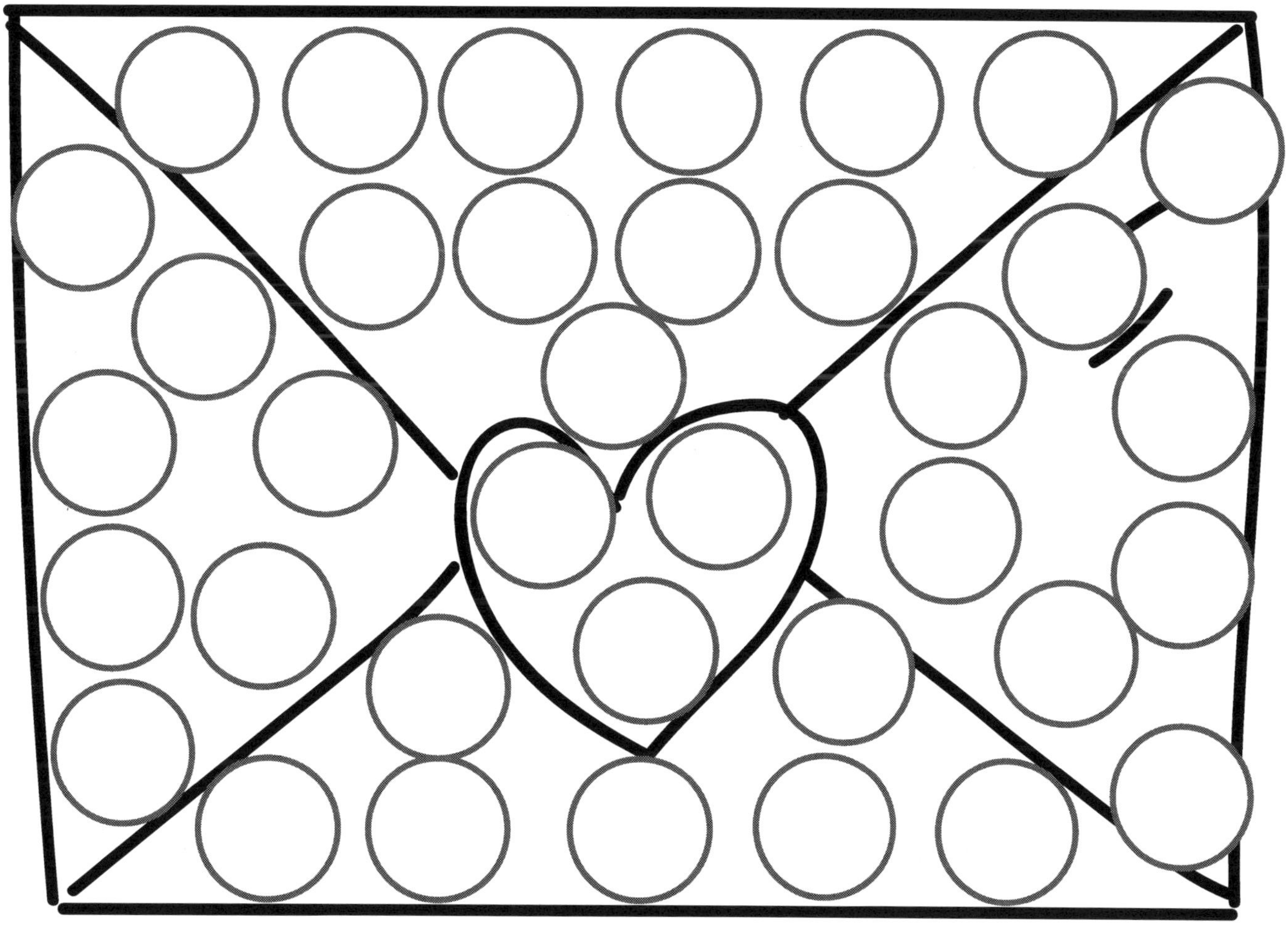

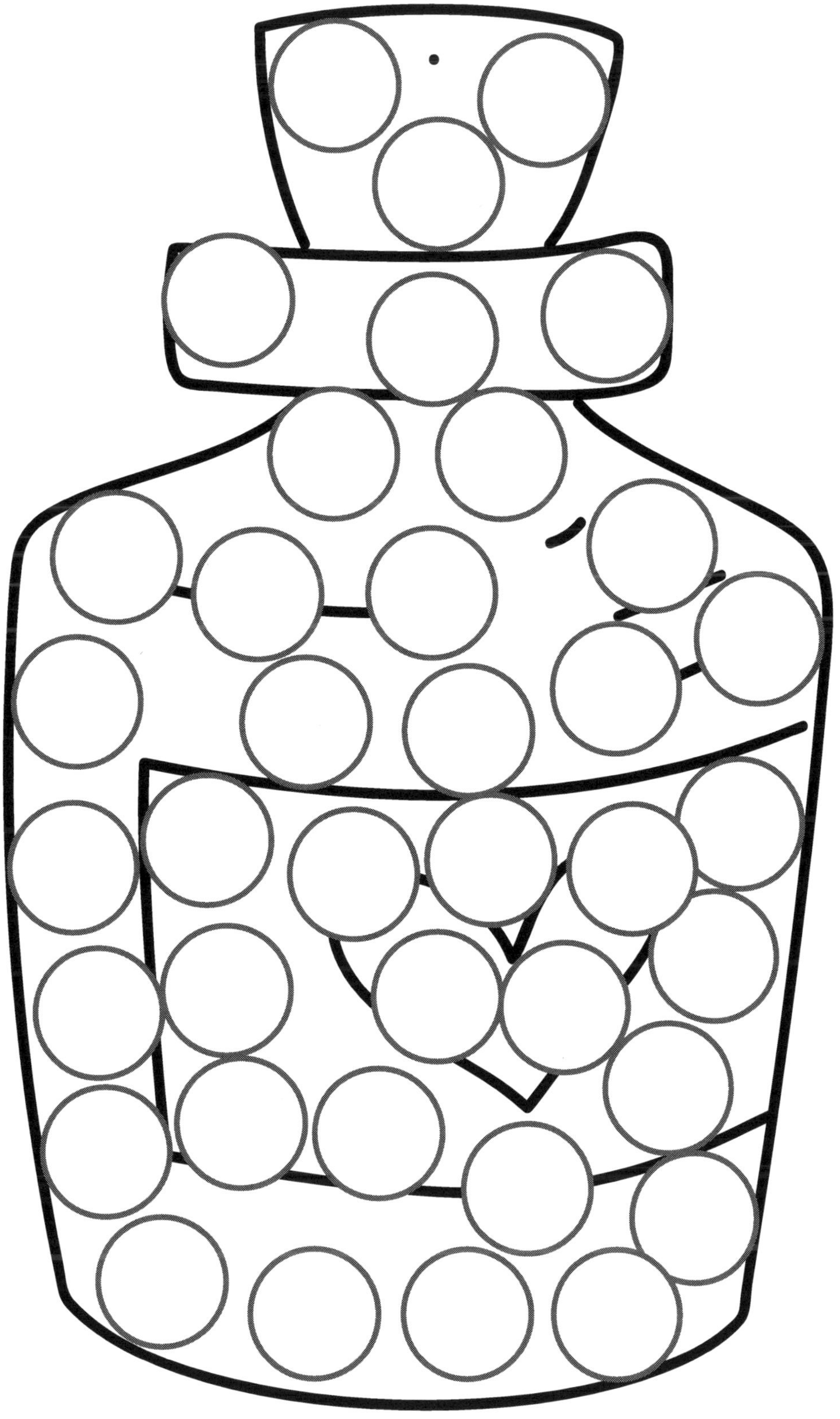

Love

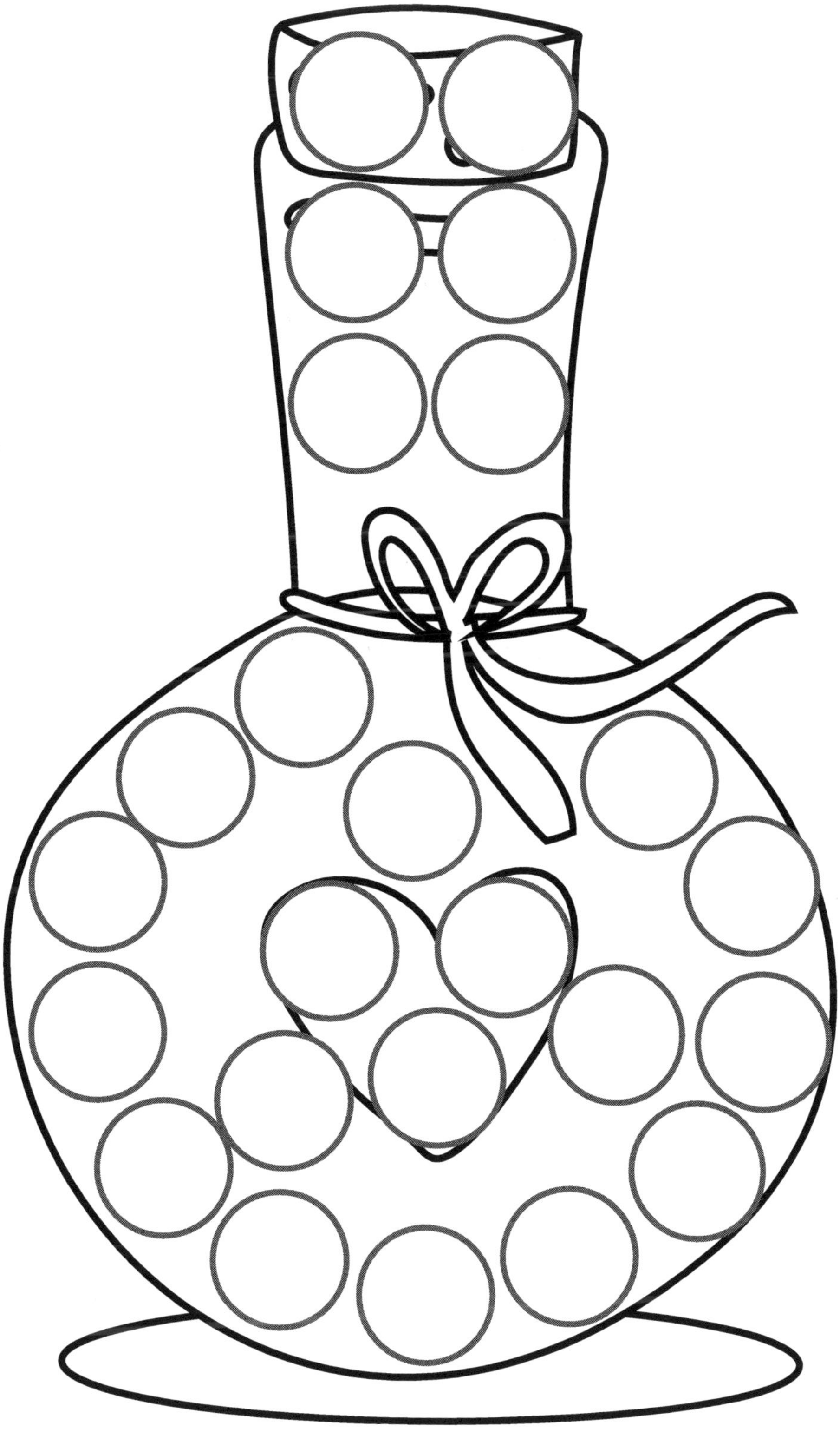

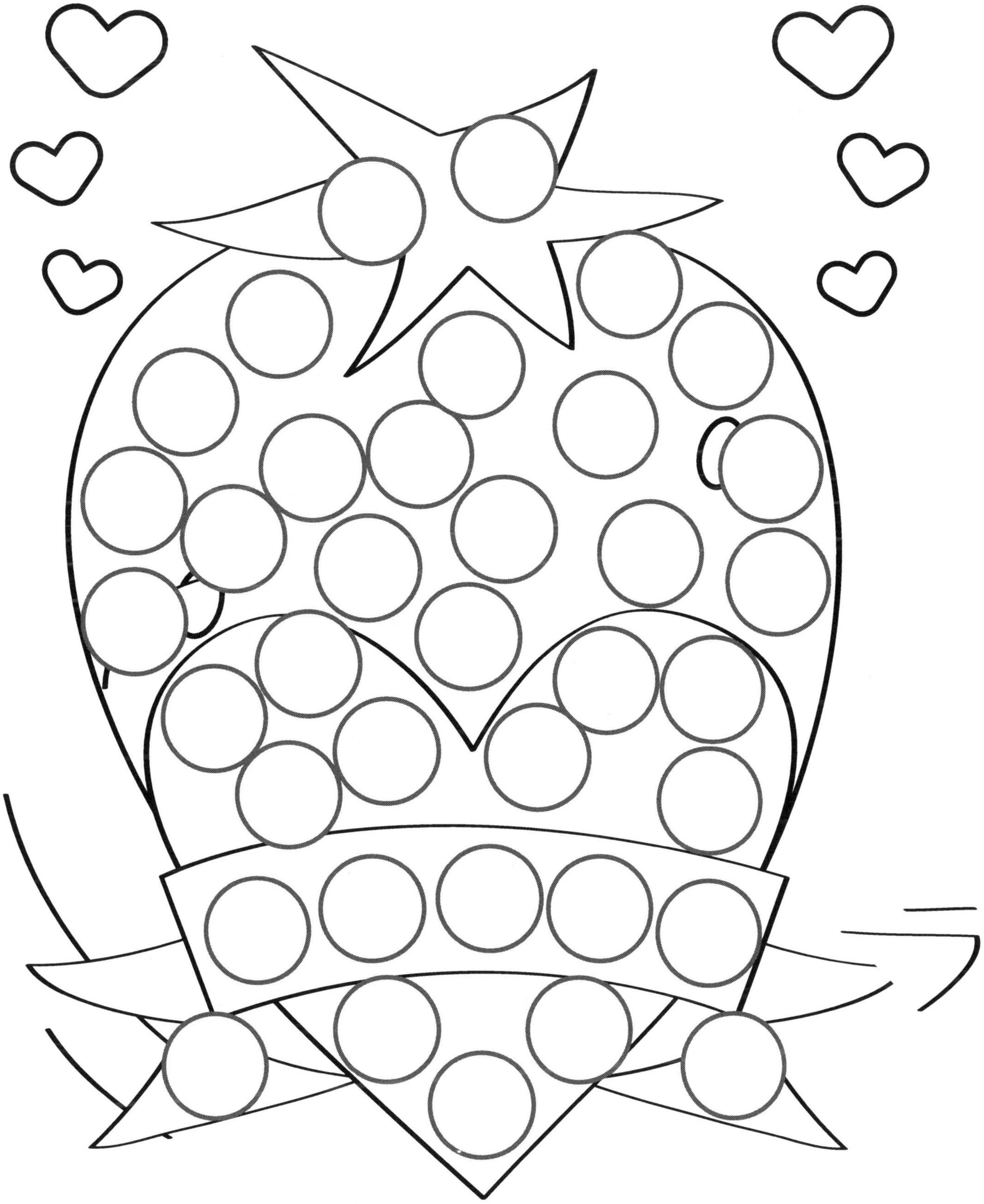

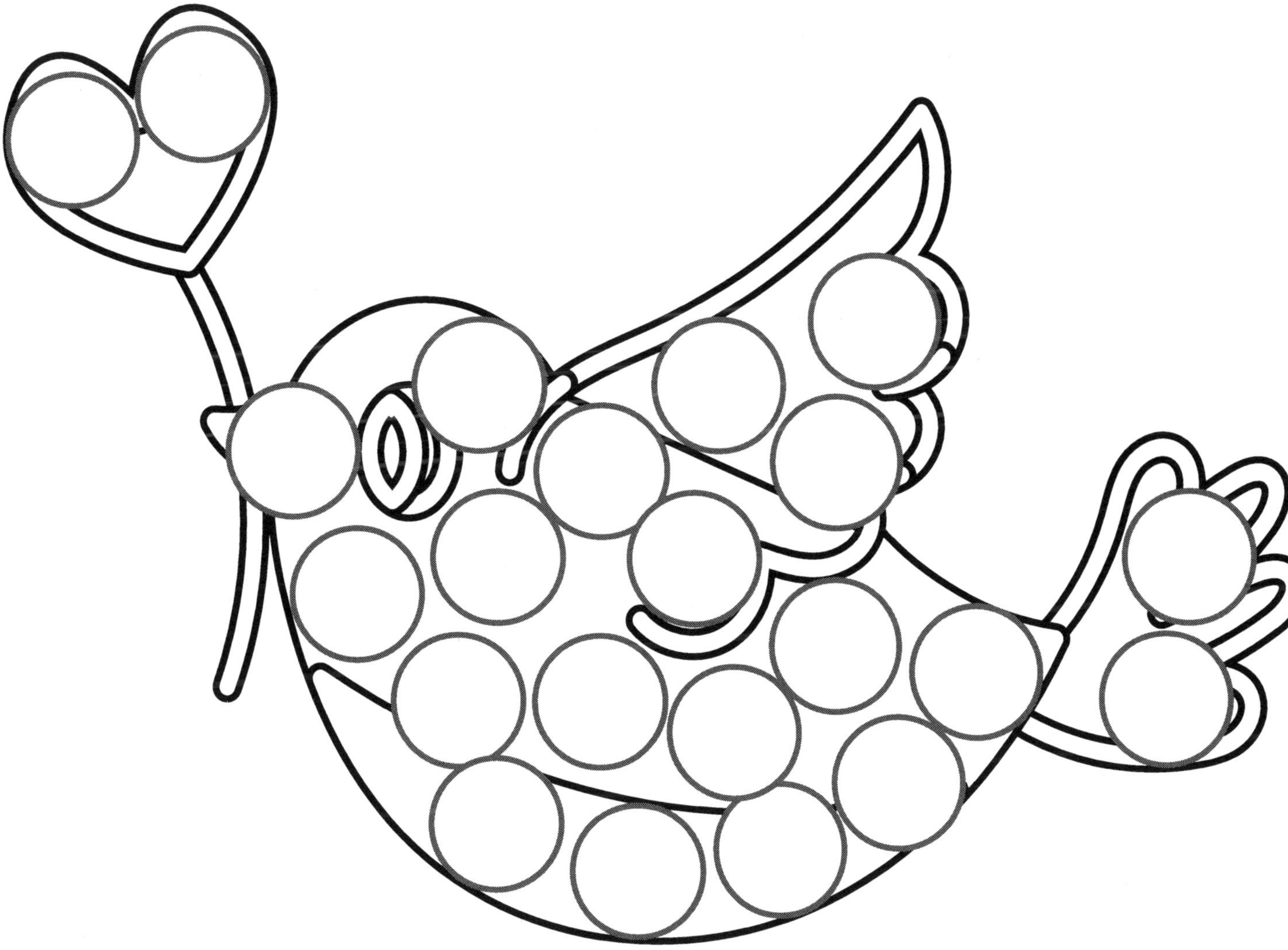

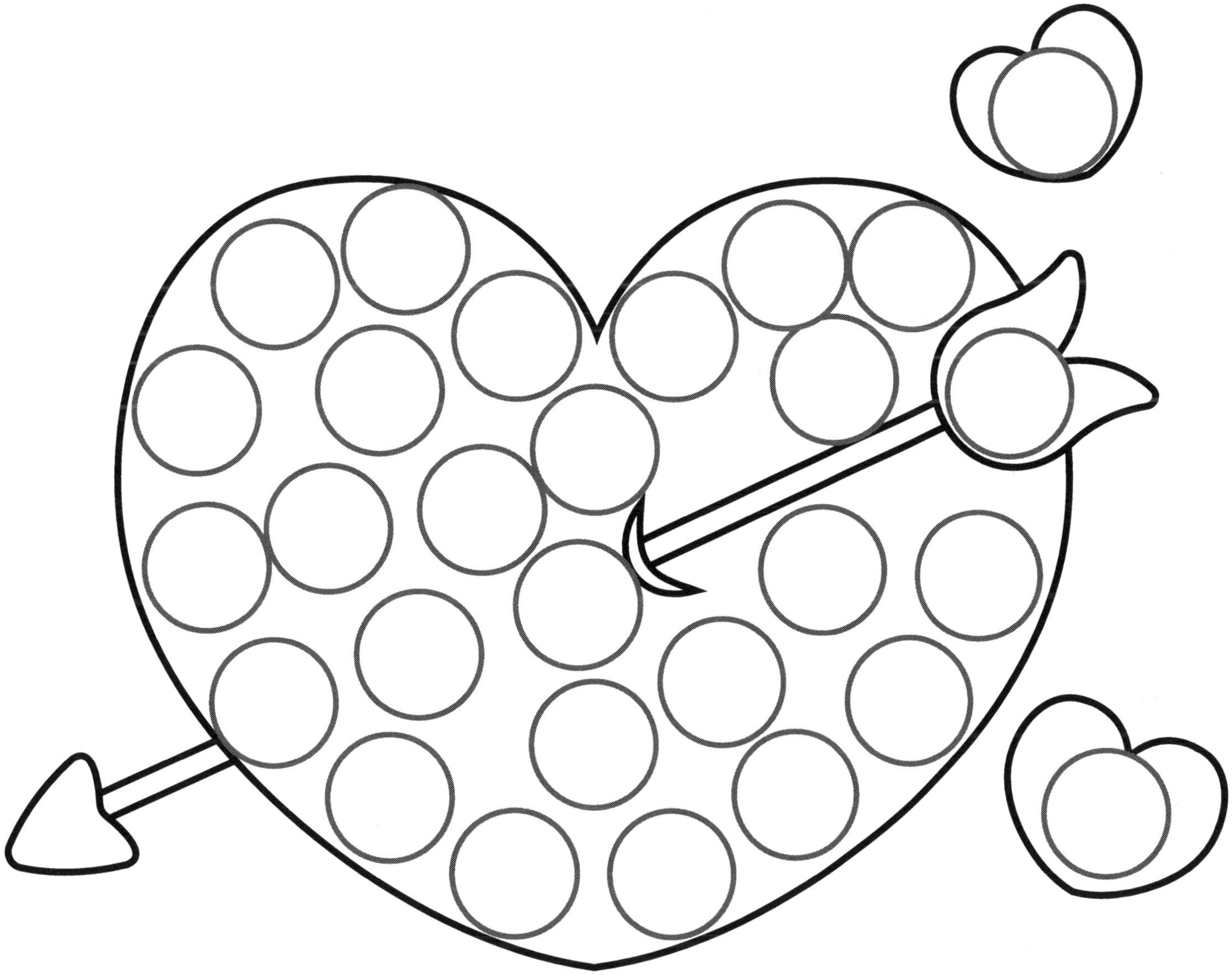

Made in the USA
Columbia, SC
08 January 2025

51488040R00054